Lysaght Surname

Ireland: 1600s to 1900s

From Ireland Church Records of Baptism, Marriage and Death

Comprised of Roman Catholic and Church of Ireland Records

From Counties Carlow, Cork, Kerry and Dublin City

Compiled by **Donovan Hurst**

March 30, 2013

Dedication

This work is dedicated to all of those that came before us and shaped our lives to make us the people that we are today.

Table of Contents

Introduction

This is a compilation of individuals who have the surname of Lysaght that lived in the country of Ireland from the 1600s to the 1900s. I have placed each entry into one of four categories: Families, Individual Births/Baptisms, Individual Burials, and Individual Marriages. If a marriage entry primarily concerns an Individual Lysaght whom is female, then I have placed that entry under the category of Individual Marriages. If a marriage entry primarily concerns an Individual Lysaght whom is male, then I have placed that entry under the category of Families. Images of many of these listings are available at http://churchrecords.irishgenealogy.ie/churchrecords/.

To help guide the reader of this work, the format of this book is as follows:

- Main Family Entry (Husband and Wife) (Father and Mother)

  o Child of Main Family Entry, including Spouse(s) when available

    ▪ Grandchild of Main Family Entry, including Spouse(s) when available

      • Great-Grandchild of Main Family Entry, including Spouse(s) when available

(**Bolded Text**) following any entry includes any additional information such as Residence(s), Occupation(s), Signature(s), etc. when available.

Hurst

Some of the fonts used in this work symbolizes Celtic writing. The traditional letters, numbers, and punctuation marks and their Celtic counterparts are as follows:

Traditional Letters (Uppercase & Lowercase)

A a B b C c D d E f G g H h I i J j K k L l M m N n O o P p Q q R r S s T t U u V v W w X x Y y Z z

Celtic Letters (Uppercase & Lowercase)

A a B b C c D ð E e F f G g H h I i J j K k L l M m

N n O o P p Q q R r S s T t U u V v W w X x Y y Z z

Traditional Numbers

1 2 3 4 5 6 7 8 9 10

Celtic Numbers

1 2 3 4 5 6 7 8 9 10

Traditional Punctuation

. , : ' " & - ( )

Celtic Punctuation

. , : ' " & - ( )

Parish Churches
Cork & Ross
(Roman Catholic or RC)

Cork - South Parish and Cork - SS. Peter & Paul Parish.

Dublin (Church of Ireland)

Arbour Hill Barracks Parish, Clontarf Parish, St. Anne Parish, St. George Parish, St. James Parish, St. Luke Parish, St. Mark Parish, St. Mary Parish, St. Peter Parish, and St. Stephen Parish.

Dublin (Roman Catholic or RC)

Rathmines Parish, SS. Michael & John Parish, St. Agatha Parish, St. Andrew Parish, St. Audoen Parish, St. Catherine Parish, St. James Parish, St. Lawrence Parish, St. Mary Parish, St. Mary, Donnybrook Parish, St. Mary, Haddington Road Parish, St. Mary, Pro Cathedral Parish, St. Michan Parish, and St. Nicholas Parish.

Kerry (Church of Ireland)

Kilnaughtin Parish.

Kerry (Roman Catholic or RC)

Ballybunion Parish, Ballyferriter Parish, Ballylongford Parish, Caherciveen Parish, Castleisland Parish, Castlemaine Parish, Causeway Parish, Dromtariffe Parish, Listowel Parish, and Millstreet Parish.

Families

- Daniel Lysaght & Margaret Byrne (B y r n e) – 30 Jan 1855 (Marriage, **St. Catherine Parish** (RC))

  o James Lysaght – bapt. 7 Dec 1855 (Baptism, **St. Catherine Parish** (RC))

Wedding Witnesses:

Michael McDonough & Ellen Lysaght

- Daniel Lysaght & Margaret Morrin

  o Mary Lysaght – b. 9 May 1861, bapt. 14 May 1861 (Baptism, **St. Catherine Parish** (RC))

Daniel Lysaght (father):

Residence - 6 Poole Street - May 14, 1861

- Edward Lysaght & Catherine Murphy

  o Abigail Lysaght – bapt. 14 Jan 1779 (Baptism, **St. Nicholas Parish** (RC))

- Edward Lysaght & Elizabeth Lynch

  o Nicholas Lysaght – b. 9 Nov 1809, bapt. 12 Nov 1809 (Baptism, **St. Catherine Parish** (RC))

- Edward Lysaght & Elizabeth Lysaght

  o Elizabeth Lysaght – b. 8 Jan 1820, bapt. 16 Jan 1820 (Baptism, **St. Luke Parish**)

- Edward Lysaght & Sarah Lee

  o Sarah Lysaght – bapt. 16 Apr 1820 (Baptism, **SS. Michael & John Parish** (RC))

Hurst

- Frederick Edward John Lysaght & Elizabeth Lysaght

    o Frederick George Lysaght – b. 10 Dec 1898, bapt. 26 Mar 1899 (Baptism, Clontarf Parish)

Frederick Edward John Lysaght (father):

Residence - 4 Cabra Parade, Clontarf - March 26, 1899

Occupation - Seaman - March 26, 1899

- George Lysaght & Elizabeth Lingard

    o Alexander Joseph Lysaght – b. 26 Sep 1862, bapt. 30 Sep 1862 (Baptism, Rathmines Parish (RC))

George Lysaght (father):

Residence - Grosvenor Terrace - September 30, 1862

- George Lysaght & Jennie Unknown

    o Stella Patricia Lysaght – b. 1 Nov 1909, bapt. 21 Nov 1909 (Baptism, St. Stephen Parish)

George Lysaght (father):

Residence - 63 Lower Baggot Street - November 21, 1909

Occupation - Esquire - November 21, 1909

- George Lingard Lysaght & Mary Jane Byrne (B y r n e) – 10 Aug 1875 (Marriage, St. Mary Parish (RC))

    o George John Lysaght – b. 23 Jul 1877, bapt. 2 Aug 1877 (Baptism, St. Mary, Donnybrook Parish (RC))

    o Charles Lingard Robert Lysaght – b. 9 Aug 1880, bapt. 22 Aug 1880 (Baptism, St. Mary, Donnybrook Parish (RC))

    o Oscar Walter Leo Lysaght – b. 23 Feb 1882, bapt. 5 Mar 1882 (Baptism, St. Mary, Donnybrook Parish (RC))

Lysaght Surname Ireland: 1600s to 1900s

- o Jarlath Edward Lysaght – b. 6 Jun 1883, bapt. 2 Jul 1883 (Baptism, **St. Mary, Donnybrook Parish (RC)**)

- o Ethel Mary Lysaght – b. 13 Aug 1884, bapt. 24 Aug 1884 (Baptism, **St. Mary, Donnybrook Parish (RC)**)

George Lingard Lysaght (father):

Residence - 14 Sandford Road - August 2, 1877

39 Morehampton Road, Donnybrook - August 22, 1880

22 Sandford Road, Donnybrook - March 5, 1882

July 2, 1883

7 Sandford Parade, Donnybrook - August 24, 1884

Wedding Witnesses:

Philip A. White & Mina Byrne

- George Lysaght & Unknown

  - o Georgina Lysaght (1st Marriage) & John V. Connolly

    - Thomas Joseph V. Connolly – b. 27 Sep 1879, bapt. 29 Sep 1879 (Baptism, **St. Mary, Haddington Road Parish (RC)**)

    - John Anselm Joseph Connolly – b. 18 Apr 1882, bapt. 22 Apr 1882 (Baptism, **St. Mary, Haddington Road Parish (RC)**)

John V. Connolly (son-in-law):

Residence - 67 Waterloo Road - September 29, 1879

39 Wellington Road - April 22, 1882

- o Georgina Lysaght Connolly (2nd Marriage) & John Prendergast – 5 Jan 1890 (Marriage, **St. Andrew Parish (RC)**)

Georgina Lysaght Connolly (daughter):

Residence - 68 Lower Mount Street - January 5, 1890

John Prendergast, son of John Prendergast (son-in-law):

Residence - 68 Lower Mount Street - January 5, 1890

Wedding Witnesses:

George Lysaght & Michael Gormley

- Gulielmo Lysaght & Anne M. Connolly
  - o Rudolph Mary Starpaster Joseph Lysaght – b. 11 Jan 1895, bapt. 18 Jan 1895 (Baptism, **St. Agatha Parish (RC)**)

Gulielmo Lysaght (father):

Residence - 10 St. Patrick's Terrace - January 18, 1895

- Henry Lysaght & Unknown
  - o Mary Lysaght & Thomas Eyre Powell – 14 Sep 1858 (Marriage, **St. George Parish**)

Signature:

Lysaght Surname Ireland: 1600s to 1900s

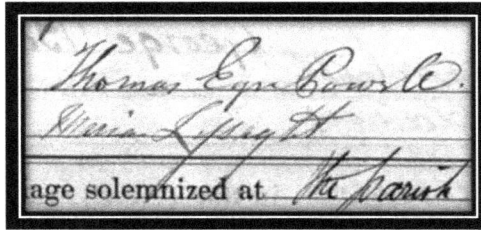

Signatures (Marriage):

Mary Lysaght (daughter):

    Residence - 7 Drumcondra Hill - September 14, 1858

Thomas Eyre Powell, son of John Powell (son-in-law):

    Residence - 26 Middle Gardiner Street - September 14, 1858

    Occupation - Esquire - September 14, 1858

John Powell (father):

    Occupation - Esquire

Henry Lysaght (father):

    Occupation - Esquire

Wedding Witnesses:

Henry Lysaght & Henry Garrett

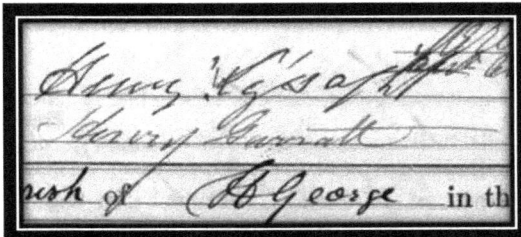

Signatures:

- o Belinda Wilhelmina Lysaght (1st Marriage) & John William Macgowan, d. bef. 8 Dec 1877 – 23 Feb 1864 (Marriage, **St. Peter Parish**)

Signatures:

- ▪ Gulielmo Henry Macgowan – b. 16 Jan 1865, bapt. 18 Jun 1889 (Baptism, **St. Mary, Donnybrook Parish (RC)**)

Gulielmo Henry Macgowan (son):

Residence - 20 Charleston Avenue - June 18, 1889

Belinda Wilhelmina Lysaght (daughter):

Residence - 3 Foster Place, St. Andrew Parish - February 23, 1864

66 Blessington Street, Dublin - February 23, 1864

John William Macgowan, son of William Macgowan (son-in-law):

Residence - 52 Ranelagh - February 23, 1864

Occupation - Builder - February 23, 1864

Relationship Status at Marriage - minor

William Macgowan (father):

Occupation - Contractor

Lysaght Surname Ireland: 1600s to 1900s

Henry Lysaght (father):

    Occupation - Esquire

Wedding Witnesses:

Thomas Eyre Powell & Robert Staviles Hooks

Signatures:

- o   Belinda Wilhelmina Lysaght Macgowan (2nd Marriage) & Florence Thomas John Murray – 8 Dec 1877

  (Marriage, **St. Peter Parish**)

Signatures:

Belinda Wilhelmina Lysaght Macgowan (daughter):

    Residence - 8 Charleston Avenue - December 8, 1877

    Relationship Status at 2nd Marriage - widow

Hurst

Florence Thomas John Murray, son of John Murray (son-in-law):

Residence - 14 Upper Mount Pleasant Avenue - December 8, 1877

Occupation - Commercial Clerk - December 8, 1877

John Murray (father):

Occupation - Commercial Clerk

Henry Lysaght (father):

Occupation - Gentleman

Wedding Witnesses:

Francis Robert Jameson & Arthur J. Hawksford

Signatures:

- James Lysaght & Anne Royne – 18 Feb 1822 (Marriage, Kilnaughtin Parish)

- James Lysaght & Ellen Connell
  - James Lysaght – b. 2 Aug 1846, bapt. 2 Aug 1846 (Baptism, Dromtariffe Parish (RC))

James Lysaght (father):

Residence - Dysart - August 2, 1846

Lysaght Surname Ireland: 1600s to 1900s

- James Lysaght & Mary Farrell

  o James Lysaght – b. 28 Jan 1859, bapt. 8 Feb 1859 (Baptism, **St. Catherine Parish** (RC))

James Lysaght (father):

Residence - 7 Meath Street - February 8, 1859

- John Lysaght & Catherine Deane – 16 Dec 1725 (Marriage, **St. Anne Parish**)

- John Lysaght & Deborah Cussen – 21 Feb 1860 (Marriage, **Listowel Parish** (RC))

  o Bridget Lysaght – b. 7 Nov 1860, bapt. 7 Nov 1860 (Baptism, **Listowel Parish** (RC))

  o William Lysaght – b. 2 Apr 1862, bapt. 2 Apr 1862 (Baptism, **Listowel Parish** (RC))

John Lysaght (father):

Residence - Listowel - February 21, 1860

November 7, 1860

April 2, 1862

Wedding Witnesses:

James Connor & Jeremiah Lyne

- John Lysaght & Elizabeth Unknown

  o Elizabeth Lysaght – bapt. 20 Aug 1783 (Baptism, **St. Nicholas Parish** (RC))

- John Lysaght & Julian Barry

  o Edmond Lysaght – bapt. 18 Oct 1761 (Baptism, **Cork - South Parish** (RC))

- John Lysaght & Margaret Hanley – 29 Nov 1823 (Marriage, **St. Mary, Pro Cathedral Parish** (RC))

Wedding Witnesses:

Michael O'Loghlen & Richard Scott

- John Lysaght & Susan Lysaght

    o John Lysaght – bapt. 10 Oct 1839 (Baptism, **St. James Parish** (RC))

- John Lysaght & Unknown – 1 Feb 1843 (Marriage, **Ballylongford Parish** (RC))

Wedding Witnesses:

James Farrell

- Martin Lysaght & Elizabeth Murray – 30 May 1852 (Marriage, **St. James Parish** (RC))

Wedding Witnesses:

Michael Callaghan & Esther Weir

- Michael Lysaght & Bridget Mary Dee

    o Bridget Lysaght – b. 1 Apr 1836, bapt. 1 Apr 1836 (Baptism, **Ballybunion Parish** (RC))

    o William Lysaght – b. 18 Mar 1839, bapt. 18 Mar 1839 (Baptism, **Ballybunion Parish** (RC))

Michael Lysaght (father):

Residence - Ghihard - April 1, 1836

March 18, 1839

- Michael Lysaght & Mary Murphy

    o William Lysaght – b. 17 Nov 1833, bapt. 17 Nov 1833 (Baptism, **Castleisland Parish** (RC))

Michael Lysaght (father):

Residence - Knockan - November 17, 1833

- Patrick Lysaght & Rose Unknown

    o Patrick Lysaght – bapt. 12 Mar 1820 (Baptism, **St. Audoen Parish** (RC))

Lysaght Surname Ireland: 1600s to 1900s

- Sylvester Lysaght & Helen Lovett

  o Thomas Lysaght – b. 6 Mar 1815, bapt. 6 Mar 1815 (Baptism, **Ballyferriter Parish** (RC))

Sylvester Lysaght (father):

Residence - Shannaknock - March 6, 1815

- Thomas Lysaght & Catherine Sughrue

  o John Lysaght – b. 8 Sep 1827, bapt. 8 Sep 1827 (Baptism, **Castlemaine Parish** (RC))

Thomas Lysaght (father):

Residence - Ballyngambune - September 8, 1827

- Thomas Lysaght & Catherine Unknown

  o Thoms Lysaght – b. 8 Mar 1804, bapt. 12 Mar 1804 (Baptism, **St. Peter Parish**)

- Thomas Lysaght & Julie Roache

  o Daniel O'Connell Lysaght – bapt. 17 Jul 1831 (Baptism, **Rathmines Parish** (RC))

- Thomas Lysaght & Mary Sheehan

  o John Lysaght – b. 1 Jan 1871, bapt. 2 Jan 1871 (Baptism, **Millstreet Parish** (RC))

  o Michael Lysaght – b. 2 Jan 1873, bapt. 4 Jan 1873 (Baptism, **Millstreet Parish** (RC))

  o Mary Bridget Lysaght – b. 26 Jan 1877, bapt. 28 Jan 1877 (Baptism, **Millstreet Parish** (RC))

  o Catherine Lysaght – b. 13 Apr 1879, bapt. 13 Apr 1879 (Baptism, **Millstreet Parish** (RC))

  o Helen Lysaght – b. 27 Sep 1881, bapt. 29 Sep 1881 (Baptism, **Millstreet Parish** (RC))

Hurst

Thomas Lysaght (father):

Residence - Millstreet - January 2, 1871

January 4, 1873

January 28, 1877

April 13, 1879

September 29, 1881

- Thomas Lysaght & Susan Hart – 7 Feb 1824 (Marriage, St. Mary Parish)

Signatures:

Thomas Lysaght (husband):

Residence - Roscommon, Co. Roscommon - February 7, 1824

Susan Hart (wife):

Residence - St. Mary Parish - February 7, 1824

Wedding Witnesses:

Edward Hart

Signature:

Lysaght Surname Ireland: 1600s to 1900s

- Thomas Lysaght & Unknown

  o Daniel Thomas Lysaght & Elizabeth Anne Simpson – 3 May 1853 (Marriage, **St. Peter Parish**)

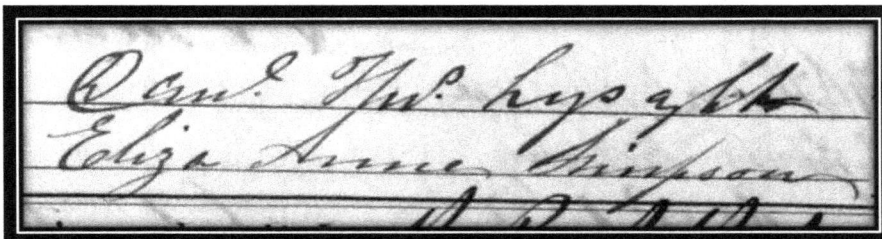

Signatures:

- Thomas John Lysaght – bapt. 4 Jun 1854 (Baptism, **Rathmines Parish (RC)**)

- James Lysaght – b. 1859, bapt. 1859 (Baptism, **St. Andrew Parish (RC)**)

Daniel Thomas Lysaght (son):

Residence - 9 Cullinswood, Ranelagh - May 3, 1853

13 Sandwith Street - 1859

Occupation - Gentleman - May 3, 1853

Elizabeth Anne Simpson, daughter of John Simpson (daughter-in-law):

Residence - Old Kilmainham - May 3, 1853

John Simpson (father):

Occupation - Esquire

Thomas Lysaght (father):

Occupation - Esquire

Hurst

Wedding Witnesses:

Thomas Cane & James Simpson

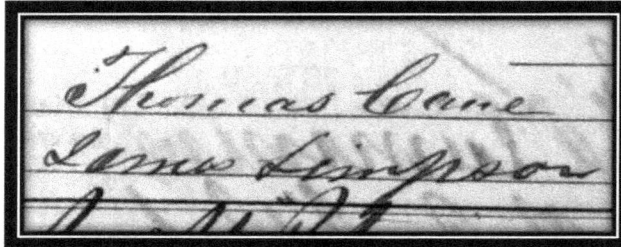

Signatures:

- Unknown Lysaght & Unknown

  o Unknown Lysaght & Frances O'Callaghan (1st Marriage)

  o Frances O'Callaghan Lysaght (2nd Marriage) & William Claudins Clifford – 31 May 1864 (Marriage, **St. Mary Parish**)

Signatures:

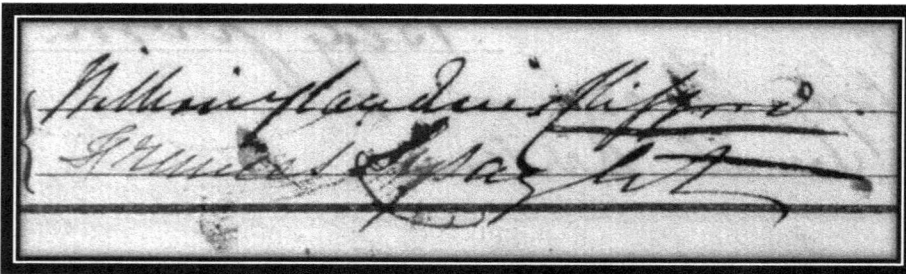

Frances O'Callaghan Lysaght, daughter of George D. O'Callaghan (wife):

Residence - 2 Charles Street - May 31, 1864

Relationship Status at 2nd Marriage - widow

Lysaght Surname Ireland: 1600s to 1900s

William Claudins Clifford, son of William Henry Clifford (husband):

    Residence - 18 Blessington Street - May 31, 1864

    Occupation - Gentleman - May 31, 1864

    Relationship Status at Marriage - widow

William Henry Clifford (father):

    Occupation - Captain, 1st [unclear] Light Calvary

George D. O'Callaghan (father):

    Occupation - Gentleman

Wedding Witnesses:

John Piercy & Elizabeth Piercy

Signatures:

- Unknown Lysaght & Unknown

  o George Lysaght

Signature:

- Unknown Lysaght & Unknown

  o Thomas Lysaght

Signature:

- William Lysaght & Margaret Leonard

  o Patrick Lysaght & Unknown Byrne (B y r n e) – 16 Feb 1904 (Marriage, **St. Mary, Pro Cathedral Parish (RC)**)

Patrick Lysaght (son):

Residence - 16 North Gloucester Place - February 16, 1904

Unknown Byrne, daughter of James Byrne & Bridget Anderson (daughter-in-law):

Residence - 11 Eden Quay - February 16, 1904

Wedding Witnesses:

Joseph Kinahan & Catherine Barker

Lysaght Surname Ireland: 1600s to 1900s

- William Lysaght & Unknown

  o Thomas Lysaght & Matilda Elizabeth Benison – 15 Mar 1849 (Marriage, **St. Peter Parish**)

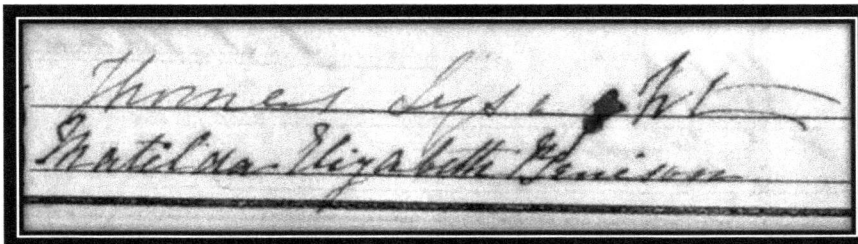

Signatures:

Thomas Lysaght (son):

   Residence - 6 Upper Baggot Street - March 15, 1849

   Occupation - Medical Doctor - March 15, 1849

   Relationship Status at Marriage - widow

Matilda Elizabeth Benison, daughter of Joseph Benison (daughter-in-law):

   Residence - 3 Tabbot Street, St. Thomas Parish - March 15, 1849

Joseph Benison (father):

   Occupation - Lieutenant in the Army

William Lysaght (father):

   Occupation - Barrister at Law

Hurst

Wedding Witnesses:

Henry Matthew John Bowles & James S. Smith

Signatures:

- William Lysaght & Unknown
  - William Lysaght & Frances Susanna Murphy – 7 May 1850 (Marriage, **St. Peter Parish**)

Signatures:

- Frances Louisa Lysaght – b. 26 May 1851, bapt. 27 Jun 1851 (Baptism, **St. Stephen Parish**)

William Lysaght (son):

Residence - 10 Percy Place - May 7, 1850

10 Mespil Parade - June 27, 1851

Occupation - Esquire - May 7, 1850

Frances Murphy, daughter of William Murphy (daughter-in-law):

Residence - 10 Mespil Parade - May 7, 1850

Lysaght Surname Ireland: 1600s to 1900s

William Murphy (father):

    Occupation - Medical Doctor

William Lysaght (father):

    Occupation - Esquire

Wedding Witnesses:

E. A. Murphy & Edward Lysaght

Signatures:

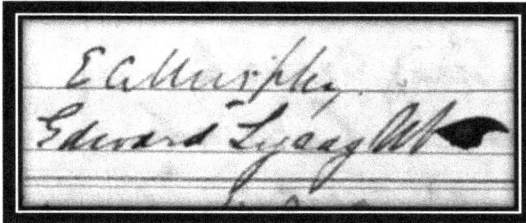

Individual Baptisms/Births

None Were Listed

Individual Burials

- Catherine Lysaght – bur. 4 Dec 1781 (Burial, **St. Mark Parish**)

- Catherine Lysaght – b. 1801, bur. 7 Apr 1834 (Burial, **St. Peter Parish**)

Catherine Lysaght (deceased):

>   Residence - Baggot Street - before April 7, 1834

>   Age at Death - 33 years

>   Place of Burial - St. Peter's Cemetery

- Edward Lysaght – bur. 30 Jul 1778 (Burial, **St. Mark Parish**)

- Mary Lysaght – bur. Dec 1811 (Burial, **St. Peter Parish**)

Mary Lysaght (deceased):

>   Residence - Stephen's Green - before December 1811

- Mary Lysaght – bur. 16 Jan 1820 (Burial, **St. James Parish**)

Mary Lysaght (deceased):

>   Residence - Bride Street - before January 16, 1820

Hurst

- Mary Lysaght – b. Jun 1859, d. 1 Dec 1859, bur. 2 Dec 1859 (Burial, **Arbour Hill Barracks Parish**)

Mary Lysaght (deceased):

 Age at Death - 6 months

 Cause of Death - Bronchitis

 Remarks - Father was in 2ⁿᵈ Battalion, 20ᵗʰ Regiment

- Unknown Lysaght – bur. 4 Feb 1809 (Burial, **St. Peter Parish**)

Unknown Lysaght (deceased):

 Residence - Leeson Street - before February 4, 1809

- Samuel Lysaght – d. 17 Aug 1827, bur. 1827 (Burial, **St. James Parish**)

Samuel Lysaght (deceased):

 Residence - Rathmines - August 17, 1827

Individual Marriages

- Anne Lysaght & William Sheridan

  - Thomas Sheridan – bapt. 24 Sep 1838 (Baptism, **Cork - South Parish** (RC))

  - Michael Sheridan – bapt. 4 Mar 1844 (Baptism, **Cork - South Parish** (RC))

- Catherine Lysaght & Daniel Herlihy

  - John Herlihy – b. 11 Jul 1876, bapt. 16 Jul 1876 (Baptism, **Cork - South Parish** (RC))

- Catherine Lysaght & John Mooney – 21 Sep 1851 (Marriage, **St. Michan Parish** (RC))

Wedding Witnesses:

James Moore & Christopher Timmins

- Catherine Lysaght & Thomas Casey

  - Helen Casey – b. 6 Dec 1902, bapt. 7 Dec 1902 (Baptism, **Caherciveen Parish** (RC))

  - Catherine Casey – b. 15 Feb 1905, 16 Feb 1905 (Baptism, **Caherciveen Parish** (RC))

Thomas Casey (father):

Residence - Caherciveen - December 7, 1902

February 16, 1905

- Charlotte Lysaght & Thomas Keogh

  - Thomas Michael Keogh – b. 22 Sep 1867, bapt. 25 Sep 1867 (Baptism, **St. Mary, Pro Cathedral Parish** (RC))

  - Catherine Margaret Keogh – b. 6 Feb 1870, bapt. 9 Feb 1870 (Baptism, **St. Lawrence Parish** (RC))

Thomas Keogh (father):

Residence - 25 Mabbot Street - September 25, 1867

2 Jane Place - February 9, 1870

- Eleanor Lysaght & Michael Finucane

  - Michael Finucane & Bridget Skeyne – 11 Jul 1869 (Marriage, **Rathmines Parish** (RC))

Michael Finucane (son):

Residence - Limerick - July 11, 1869

Bridget Skeyne, daughter of Michael Skeyne & Margaret Ward (daughter-in-law):

Residence - Leinster Square - July 11, 1869

Wedding Witnesses:

Thomas F. O'Neil & Nora Skeyne

- Eleanor Lysaght & Thomas Dyer

  - John Dyer – b. 8 Dec 1867, bapt. 9 Dec 1867 (Baptism, **St. Michan Parish** (RC))

Thomas Dyer (father):

Residence - 4 New Lisburn Street - December 9, 1867

- Elizabeth Lysaght & Michael O'Donnell

  - Elizabeth O'Donnell – b. 3 Jan 1871, bapt. 8 Jan 1871 (Baptism, **Cork - SS. Peter & Paul Parish** (RC))

Lysaght Surname Ireland: 1600s to 1900s

- Elizabeth Lysaght & Patrick Hynes – 5 Dec 1852 (Marriage, **St. Andrew Parish** (RC))

Wedding Witnesses:

John Keegan & Anne Murray

- Ellen Lysaght & Daniel Barry – 11 Jun 1797 (Marriage, **Cork - South Parish** (RC))

  o John Barry – bapt. 27 Feb 1800 (Baptism, **Cork - South Parish** (RC))

Daniel Barry (father):

  Residence - Mac [unclear] - **February 27, 1800**

Wedding Witnesses:

David Barry & Timothy Jones

- Frances Lysaght & James Healy

  o James Healy – bapt. 29 Apr 1784 (Baptism, **St. Nicholas Parish** (RC))

  o Michael Healy – bapt. 6 Nov 1786 (Baptism, **St. Nicholas Parish** (RC))

- Jane Lysaght & Daniel Donahy

  o James Donahy – bapt. 29 May 1774 (Baptism, **Cork - SS. Peter & Paul Parish** (RC))

  o Daniel Donahy – bapt. 17 Mar 1776 (Baptism, **Cork - SS. Peter & Paul Parish** (RC))

- Joan Lysaght & Daniel Riordan

  o Michael Riordan – b. 2 Jan 1871, bapt. 3 Jan 1871 (Baptism, **Millstreet Parish** (RC))

  o Mary Riordan – b. 9 Jan 1872, bapt. 10 Jan 1872 (Baptism, **Millstreet Parish** (RC))

  o Julie Riordan – b. 16 Feb 1873, bapt. 18 Feb 1873 (Baptism, **Millstreet Parish** (RC))

  o Honor Riordan – b. 22 Apr 1875, bapt. 23 Apr 1875 (Baptism, **Millstreet Parish** (RC))

  o Daniel Riordan – b. 6 May 1876, bapt. 7 May 1876 (Baptism, **Millstreet Parish** (RC))

Hurst

- o Mary Riordan – b. 17 Mar 1877, bapt. 19 Mar 1877 (Baptism, **Millstreet Parish** (RC))

- o Patrick Riordan – b. 1 Nov 1878, bapt. 3 Nov 1878 (Baptism, **Millstreet Parish** (RC))

- o Ellen Riordan – b. 4 Aug 1880, bapt. 5 Aug 1880 (Baptism, **Millstreet Parish** (RC))

- o William Riordan – b. 8 Sep 1881, bapt. 11 Sep 1881 (Baptism, **Millstreet Parish** (RC))

- o Joan Riordan – b. 17 Sep 1882, bapt. 18 Sep 1882 (Baptism, **Millstreet Parish** (RC))

Daniel Riordan (father):

Residence - Cullen - January 3, 1871

January 10, 1872

February 18, 1873

April 23, 1875

May 7, 1876

March 19, 1877

November 3, 1878

August 5, 1880

September 11, 1881

September 18, 1882

- Margaret Lysaght & Bartholomew Brown

  - o John Brown – b. 1 Feb 1836, bapt. 1 Feb 1836 (Baptism, **Causeway Parish** (RC))

  - o Nicholas Brown – b. 24 Jun 1838, bapt. 24 Jun 1838 (Baptism, **Causeway Parish** (RC))

Lysaght Surname Ireland: 1600s to 1900s

Bartholomew Brown (father):

Residence - Clihane - February 1, 1836

June 24, 1838

- Margaret Lysaght & Westby Perceval – 9 Aug 1817 (Marriage, **St. Peter Parish**)

Margaret Lysaght (wife):

Residence - St. Peter Parish - August 9, 1817

Westby Perceval (husband):

Residence - St. Peter Parish - August 9, 1817

Wedding Witnesses:

Thomas Lysaght & David Lysaght

- Mary Lysaght & Beverly Ussher – 26 Mar 1733 (Marriage, **St. Peter Parish**)

Beverly Ussher (husband):

Residence - Consistory Court - March 26, 1733

- Mary Lysaght & James Goggin
  - Catherine Goggin – b. 12 Nov 1809, bapt. 12 Nov 1809 (Baptism, **Ballyferriter Parish** (RC))
  - Unknown Goggin – b. 22 Aug 1816, bapt. 22 Aug 1816 (Baptism, **Ballyferriter Parish** (RC))

James Goggin (father):

Residence - Riasque - November 12, 1809

Ballineanag - August 22, 1816

- Mary Lysaght & John Dalton

  o Thomas Dalton – b. 10 Jan 1836, bapt. 10 Jan 1836 (Baptism, **Causeway Parish** (RC))

John Dalton (father):

Residence - Causeway - January 10, 1836

- Mary Lysaght & Lawrence O'Callaghan

  o Jeremiah O'Callaghan – b. 20 Jan 1870, bapt. 21 Jan 1870 (Baptism, **Millstreet Parish** (RC))

  o Margaret O'Callaghan – b. 16 Jan 1872, bapt. 18 Jan 1872 (Baptism, **Millstreet Parish** (RC))

  o Catherine O'Callaghan – b. 21 Aug 1874, bapt. 22 Aug 1874 (Baptism, **Millstreet Parish** (RC))

  o Mary O'Callaghan – b. 4 Feb 1877, bapt. 4 Feb 1877 (Baptism, **Millstreet Parish** (RC))

Lawrence O'Callaghan (father):

Residence - Millstreet - January 21, 1870

January 18, 1872

August 22, 1874

February 4, 1877

- Mary Lysaght & Michael Finnegan

  o Catherine Finnegan – bapt. 2 Nov 1801 (Baptism, **St. Catherine Parish** (RC))

- Mary Lysaght & Thomas Murphy

  o Thomas Murphy – b. 11 Nov 1850, bapt. 11 Nov 1850 (Baptism, **Causeway Parish** (RC))

Thomas Murphy (father):

Residence - Causeway - November 11, 1850

Lysaght Surname Ireland: 1600s to 1900s

- Mary Lysaght & William Cleary Keys – 22 Oct 1838 (Marriage, **St. Mary Parish**)

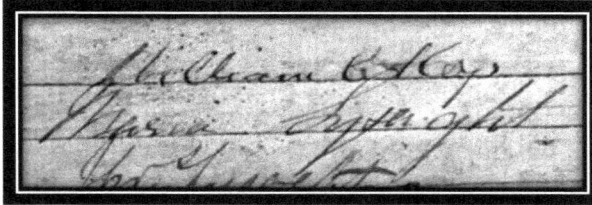

Signatures:

Mary Lysaght (wife):

Residence - St. Mary Parish - October 22, 1838

William Cleary Keys (husband):

Residence - St. Mary Parish - October 22, 1838

Wedding Witnesses:

Thomas Lysaght & John Orpin

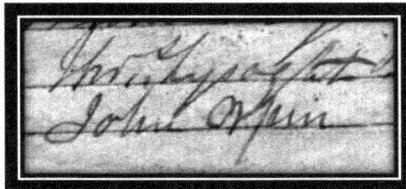

Signatures:

- Mary Victoria Lysaght & George Plunkett – 8 Jan 1840 (Marriage, **St. Mary, Pro Cathedral Parish (RC)**)

Wedding Witnesses:

Thomas Lysaght & Elizabeth Fitzgerald

Hurst

- Sarah Lysaght & William Teare – 5 Dec 1832 (Marriage, **St. Peter Parish**)

Sarah Lysaght (wife):

    Residence - Longford Street, St. Peter Parish - December 5, 1832

    Occupation - Spinster - December 5, 1832

William Teare (husband):

    Residence - Longford Street, St. Peter Parish - December 5, 1832

Wedding Witnesses:

Thomas Lysaght & Margaret Brett

- Sarah Ludovica Lysaght & John Kelly
  - Catherine Mary Kelly – bapt. 19 Aug 1834 (Baptism, **St. Michan Parish (RC)**)

Name Variations

Includes Latin and Abbreviated forms of names found in the original documents.

Abigail = Abigale, Abigall

Anne = Ann, Anna, Annae

Bartholomew = Barth, Bartholmeus, Bartholomeo

Bridget = Birgis, Brigid, Brigida, Bridgit

Catherine = Catharine, Catharina, Catharinae, Catherina, Cath, Catha, Cathae, Cathe, Cathn, Kate

Charles = Carolus, Charls, Chas

Christopher = Christoph

Daniel = Danielem, Danielis

Edmund = Edmond

Edward = Ed, Edwd

Eleanor = Eleo, Eleonora, Elinor, Ellenor

Elizabeth = Betty, Elisa, Elisabeth, Eliz, Eliza, Elizab, Elizh, Elizth

Ellen = Elena, Ellena

Emily = Emilia

Esther = Essie, Ester

Francis = Fransicum

George = Geo, Georg, Georgius

Grace = Gratiae

Gulielmo = Guil, Guillelmi, Gulielmum, Guillelmus, Gulmi

Helen = Helena

Lysaght Surname Ireland: 1600s to 1900s

Honor = Hanora, Honora

James = Jacobi, Jacobus, Jas

Jane = Joanna

Jeanne = Jeannae, Joannae

Joan = Johanna, Joney

John = Jno, Joannem, Joannes, Johannis

Joseph = Jos

Juliana = Julian

Leticia = Letitia, Lettice, Letticia

Lewis = Louis

Luke = Lucas

Margaret = Margarita, Margaritae, Margeret, Marget, Margt

Martha = Marthae

Mary = Maria, My

Mary Anne = Marianna, Marianne, Maryanne

Michael = Michaelis, Michl

Patrick = Pat, Patt, Patk, Patricii, Patricius

Peter = Petri

Richard = Ricardi, Ricardus, Rich, Richd

Robert = Roberti

Rose = Rosa, Rosae

Thomas = Thom, Thomae, Thoms, Thos, Ths

Timothy = Timotheus, Timy

William = Wil, Will, Willm, Wm

Notes

Notes

Notes

Notes

Notes

Notes

Index

D

F

G

H

Hurst

M

About The Author

Donovan Hurst graduated from San Diego State University with a Bachelor of Arts in the major field of studies of History and a minor in the field of studies of Anthropology. He is a current member of The General Society of Mayflower Descendants and has been conducting genealogical research for over 10 years tracing back his ancestors to their ancestral homelands in Denmark, England, France, Germany, Ireland, Norway, and Scotland.

www.ingramcontent.com/pod-product-compliance
Lightning Source LLC
Chambersburg PA
CBHW081203270326
41930CB00014B/3274